Your Journey is a Dream

Calligraphy
by
Michael Strong

Poems
by
Christina Starobin

Michael dedicates this book to Christina

Christina dedicates this book to Michael

Reader, you may dedicate this book to whom you wish

Contents

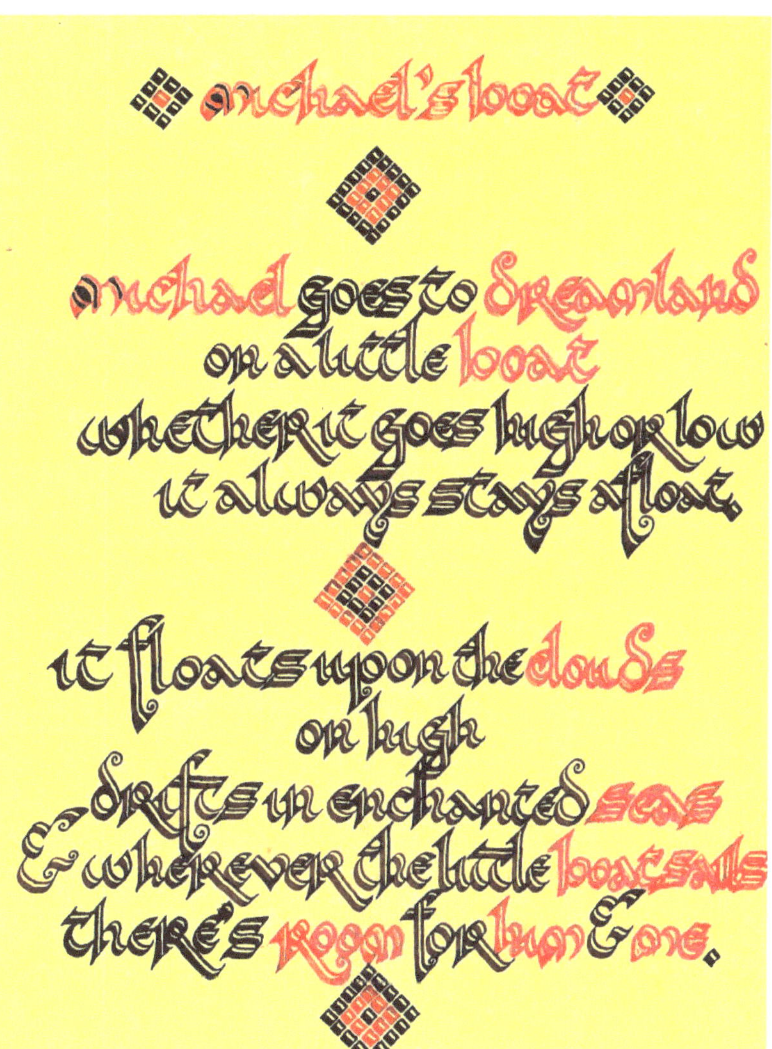
Michael's Boat

Michael goes to dreamland
on a little boat
whether it goes high or low
it always stays afloat.

it floats upon the clouds
on high
drifts in enchanted seas
& wherever the little boat sails
there's room for him & one.

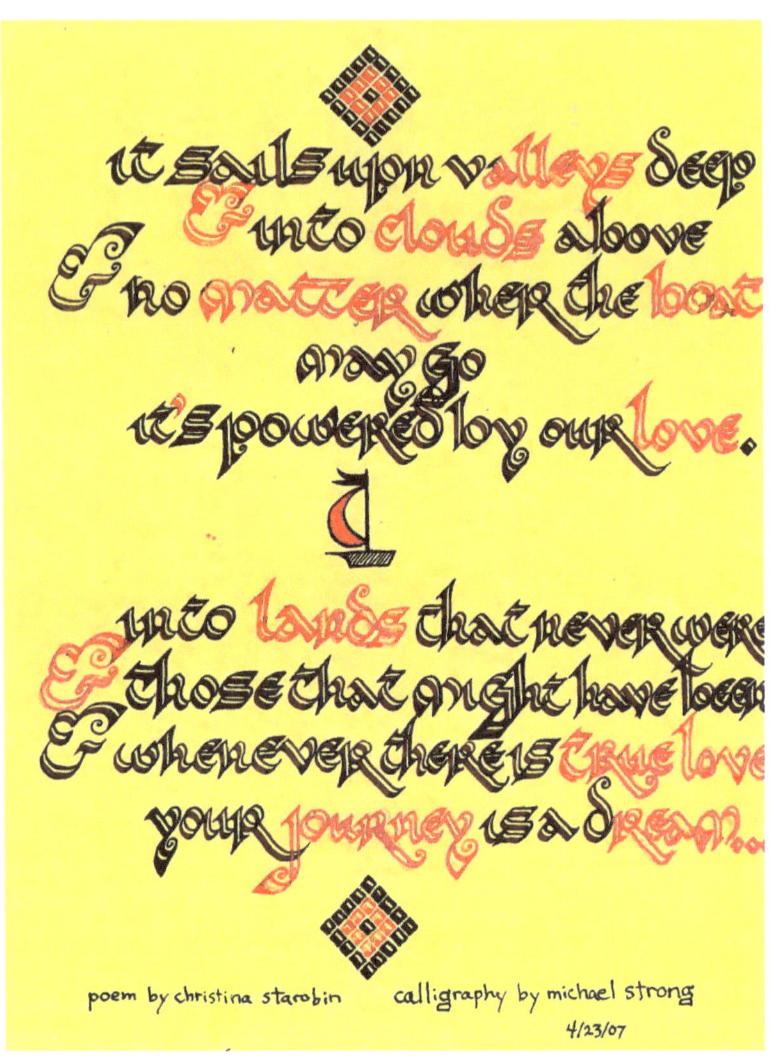
it sails upon valleys deep
& into clouds above
& no matter where the boat may go
it's powered by our love.

unto lands that never were
& those that might have been
& whenever there is true love
your journey is a dream...

poem by christina starobin   calligraphy by michael strong
4/23/07

walking through the
snow, our morning spree
my dog
i discovered
a newly dead dead deer
an unexpected outcome
we could not foresee

the length of life is
something we can't
foresee

no matter the worth
or how we persevere

ten million tiny fossils
will outlive me

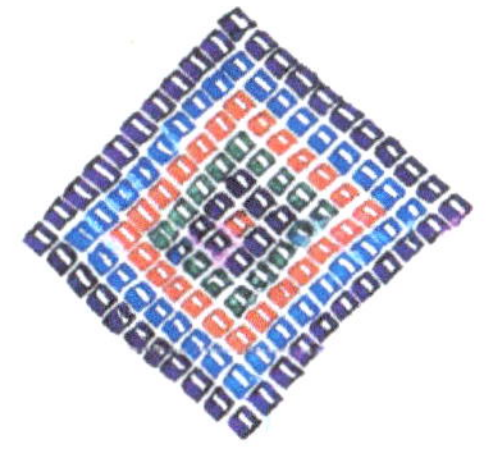

the deer had counted

not its legacy

the shot that caught it

we didn't even hear

uan unexpected

outcome we did not

foresee....

what i achieve in life
has yet to be
but one fact remains
self-evident
&
near
ten million tiny fossils
will outlive me

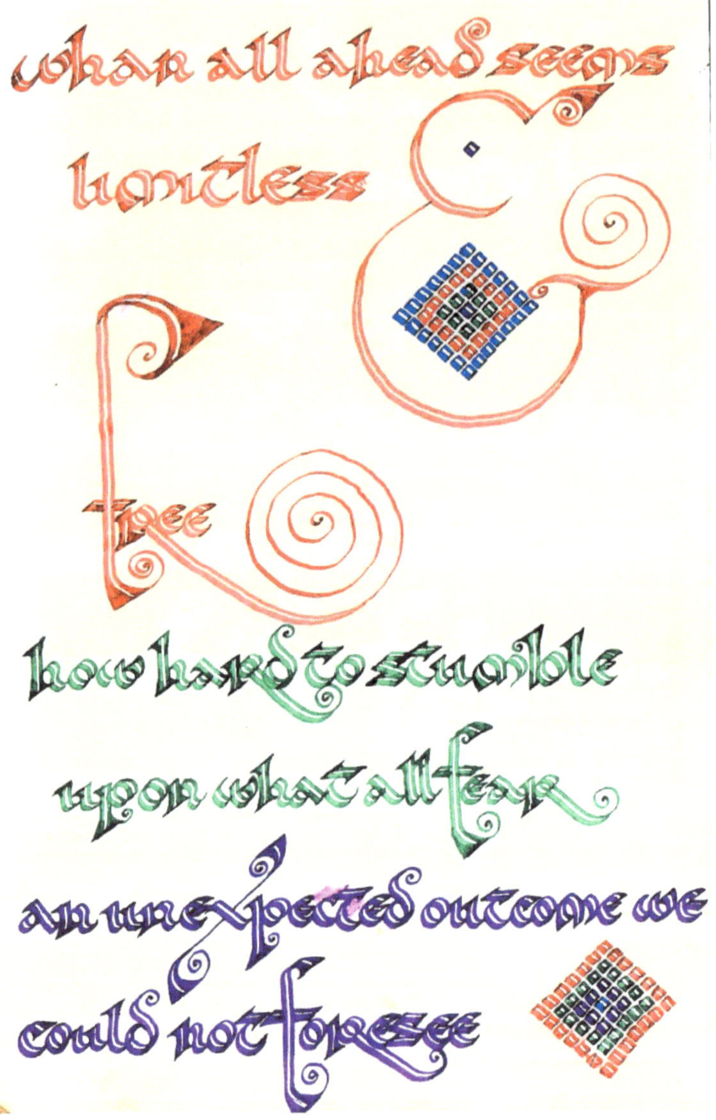
when all ahead seems
limitless
free
how hard to stumble
upon what all fear
an unexpected outcome we
could not foresee

no matter how great

my achievements be

whenever we think

we see the future clear

an unexpected outcome

we could not foresee....

ten million tiny fossils

will outlive me

feelings of hurt cannot
be forestalled

snow is warm when
sometimes friends are
cold

love keeps giving like
a waterfall

silence hides its mortar

like a wall

until you see the pattern

; then it's told

lonely like a stone

gives not at all

those who withhold
cannot obey the call

that melting over

mossy banks unfolds

love keeps giving

like a waterfall

when decat is evident
to all
standing still
turns all your dreams
to mold....
lonely like a stone
gives not at all

see here the white
where future
footsteps fall
those who hear will
not judge or scold
love keeps giving like
a waterfall

so walking by the

wilderness exiled

regain your worth

like the pines

stand tall

love keeps giving like

a waterfall

lonely

like

a

stone

gives

not

at

all

On New Year's Eve
we plan a special eve-
ning
&
we spend

on food, on tickets, clothes
to have a blast

can this night stand
alone or will it...

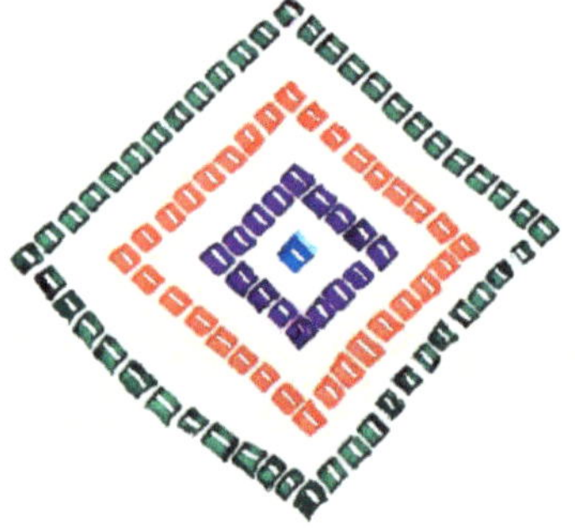

but then the fates
decide to switch & send

a snowstorm to

reverse the die we

cast

always life surprises

at the end

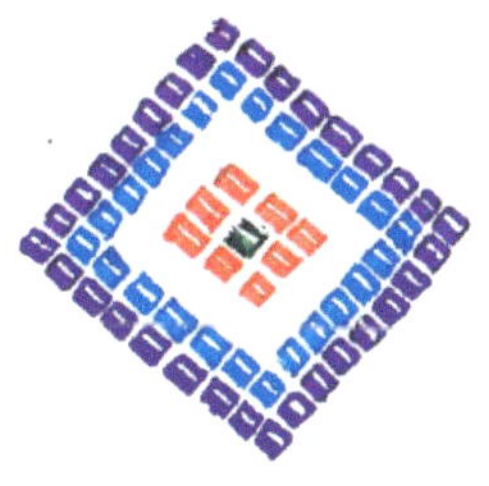

unthaw the roast;

perhaps our natures
tend

to welcome new year

with the same old cast

can this night stand

alone or will it ...
portend ?

the winds that blow the
snow around the bend
of the house, swirl
memories of all years
past
always life surprises
in the end....

how can we know our

foes from friends?

when each encompasses

both, changing fast?

can this right stand

alone,

or will it portend?

new year's eve makes

all fences mend

mystery of old turned

new triumphs at last

can this night stand

alone or will it

portend?

always life surprises....

in the end....

can we still care?

new year's snow
behind the maple tall

brown leaves still
adhere to blacker
boughs

does the leaf still sway
or does it finally fall?

If I watch & wait
through it all
will this leaf remain
with its spouse?
can we predict the
future after all?

or will it disattach
in an instant's call
the moment that i turn
inside the house?
does the leaf still sway
or
does
it
fall?

how much in fact does
our attention null
the events? if i'm an
invisible mouse
can we predict the
future after all ??

or will all the other
leaves agree to
appall
unpredictability,
motionless, so we can
grouse?

does the leaf still sway
or finally fall?

shall i turn to go or do i stall?

once gone can i this leaf reroute?

does the leaf still sway or finally fall?

can we predict the future after all?

cleaning the garage in
winter was no mistake
we need to purge this
space this
time around

time
reinvents us like a
snake

there it was:

resting behind a rake

transparent

snakeskin curled upon

the ground

we shed ourselves,

what we make, remake

there were times when

this reptile made me

quake

but a deeper wonder now

i've found

time reinvents us like

a snake

it lives beneath the

stairs beside the lake

eats its once

making not a sound

we shed ourselves,

what we make,

remake

I've seen it twice; it
shocks you quite awake

its amazing moves
cannot but astound

time reinvents us like
a snake

it used the garage as a

dressing room to make

its presence in absence

turn our thoughts around

time reinvents us like

a snake

we shed ourselves,

what we make,remake

the day starts ; the
sun clears the ground

the threat of snow makes
the sky's grey haze

where you will be when
the sun goes down?

If on your journey ever tightly wound

to gather all in your radar gaze

are you coming back from on the town?

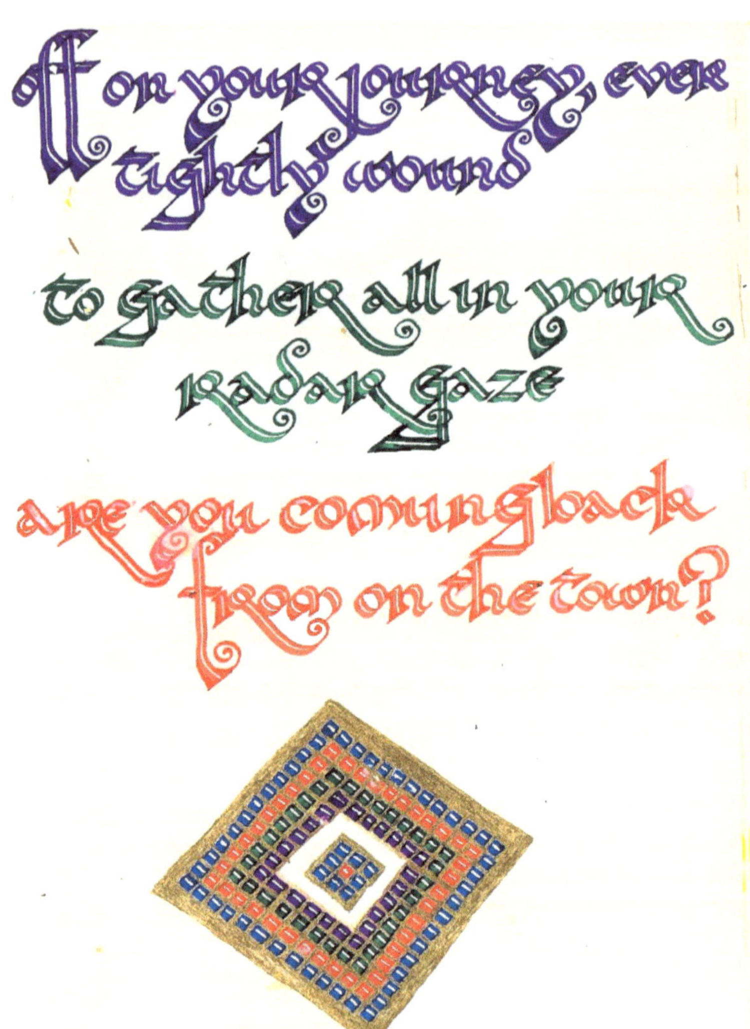

will you call & tell me what
you've found?

or leave me to my own
frenetic craze?

where will you be
when the sun
goes
down?

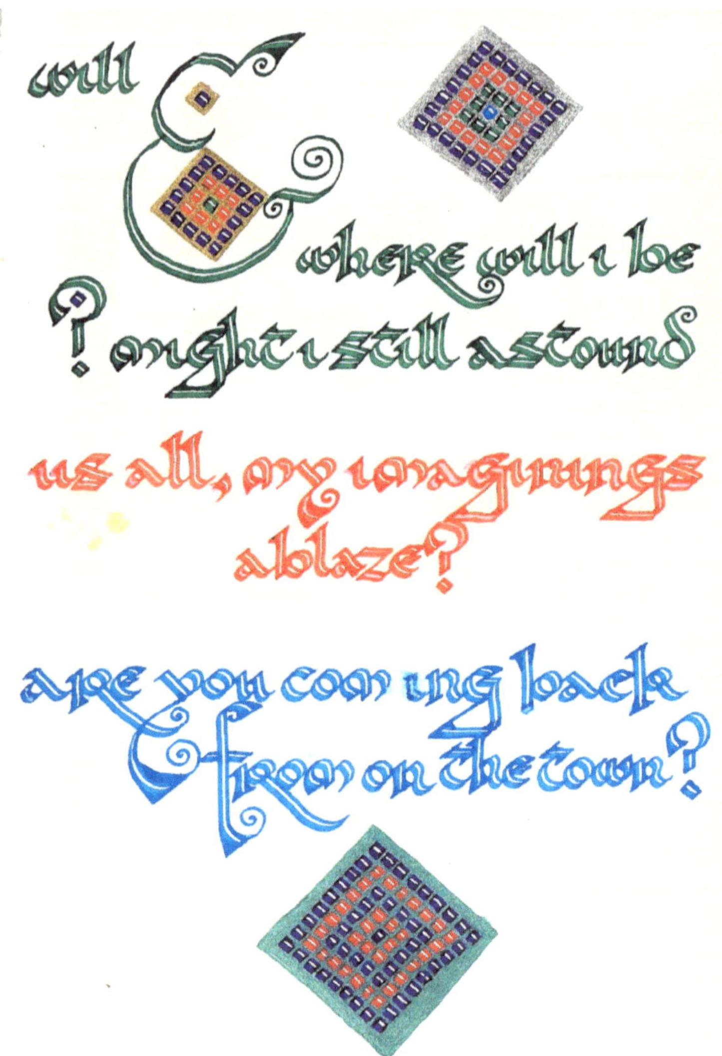

will
where will i be
? might i still astound
us all, my imaginings
ablaze?
are you coming back
from on the town?

i might scale a wall in
a single bound

or find a cure for
loneliness that
stays

where will you be
when
the sun
goes
down?

in the dark i gather
lights around
& animals to
nestle in their ways
where will you be when
the sun
goes
down?

are you coming back from on the town?

when i was young i
wished to be a cat

years later, my cat
saved me from
despair

i would have died years
ago but for that

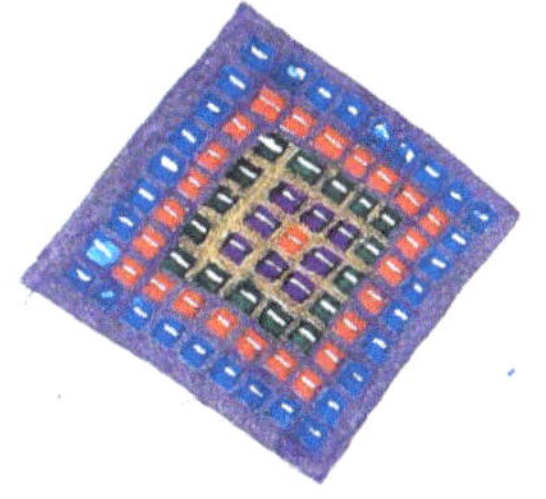

in later years, death wore a different hat

i courted danger

i never had a care

the full moon through the bedroom window~

eclat!

circumstances
intervened to make one
fat
& medicines
regimes
so rare
i would have died years
ago but for that

with gratitude forgot,
i was a rat

no cat could catch me
underneath any
chair

the full moon through
the bedroom
window:
éclat!

to those i loved i never
was a brat

put them before me,
mortged all my air

i would have died years
ago but for that

now i wait, afraid of
fortune's spats
that mangle me; i watch
it waiting there

i would have died years
ago but for that

the full moon through
the bedroom window :

eclat!

i've always been
independent

self-styled

the mainstream was a
mystery to me

was there more clarity
as a child?

as an adolescent i
sometimes dialed
the radio & thought
the music
a key

i find my imagination
cascades wild

Then when i was married & beguiled

unto thinking self-sacrifice was glee

was there more clarity as a child?

could i have prevented
horrors harsh or mild

if i had turned away
from some mad spree?

i find my imagination

cascades wild

The boss now wants me to "go the extra mile"

I know that soon they'll shoot me in the knee

was there more clarity as a child?

will i ever know if
fortune smiled

by making my choices
few & all but easy
was there more
clarity as a child?

i find my imagination

e
a
s
c
a
d
e
s wild

Michael's boat

Michael goes to dreamland
On a little boat
Whether it goes high or low
It always stays afloat

It float upon the clouds on high
Drifts in enchanted seas
& wherever the little boat sails
There's room for him & me

It sails upon valleys deep
& into clouds above
& no matter where the boat may go
It's powered by our love

Into the lands that never were
& those that might have been
& whenever there is true love
Your journey is a dream

Walking through the snow, our morning spree
My dog & I discovered a newly dead deer
An unexpected outcome we could not foresee

The length of life is something we can't foresee
No matter the worth or how we persevere
Then million tiny fossils will outlive me

The deer had counted not its legacy
The shot that caught it we didn't even hear
An unexpected outcome we did not foresee

What I achieve in life has yet to be
But one fact remains self-evident & near
Ten million tiny fossils will outlive me

When all ahead seems limitless & free
How hard to stumble upon what all fear
An unexpected outcome we could not foresee

No matter how great my achievements be
Whenever we think we see the future clear
An unexpected outcome we could not foresee
Ten million tiny fossils will outlive me

Feelings of hurt cannot be forestalled
Snow is warm when sometime friends are cold
Love keeps giving like a waterfall

Silence hides its mortar like a wall
Until you see the pattern; then it's told
Lonely like a stone gives not at all

Those who withhold cannot obey the call
That melting over mossy banks unfolds
Love keeps giving a like a waterfall

When deceit is evident to all
& standing still turns all your dreams to mold
Lonely like a stone gives not at all

See here the white where future footsteps fall
Those who hear will not judge or scold
Love keeps giving like a waterfall

So walking by the wilderness cajoled
Regain your worth & like the pines stand tall
Love keeps giving like a waterfall
Lonely like a stone gives not at all

On New Year's Eve we plan a special evening & we spend
On food, on tickets, clothes to have a blast
Can this night stand alone or will it …portend?

But then the fates decide to swiftly send
Snowstorm to reverse the die we cast
Always life surprises at the end

Unthaw the roast; perhaps our natures tend
To welcome new year with the same old cast
Can this night stand alone or will it …portend?

The winds that blow the snow around the bend
Of the house, swirl memories of all years past
Always life surprises, in the end

How can we know our foes from friends?
When each encompasses both, changing fast
Can this night stand alone, or will it portend?

New Year's Eve makes all fences mend
Mystery of old turned new triumphs at last
Can this night stand alone or will it portend?
Always life surprises in the end

Can we still care? New year's snow behind the maple tall
Brown leaves still adhere to blacker boughs
Does the leaf still sway or does it finally fall?

If I watch & wait through it all
Will this leaf remain with its spouse?
Can we predict the future after all?

Or will it disattach in an instant's call
The moment that I turn inside the house
Does the left still sway or does it fall?

How much in fact does our attention mull
The events? If I'm an invisible mouse
Can we predict the future after all?

Or will the other leaves agree to appall
Predictably, motionless, so we can grouse?
Does the leaf still sway or finally fall?

Shall I turn to go or do I stall?
Once gone can I this leaf reroute?
Does the left still sway or finally fall?
Can we predict the future after all?

Cleaning the garage in winter was no mistake
We need to purge this space this time around
Time reinvents us like a snake

& there it was: resting behind a rake
Transparent snakeskin curled upon the ground
We shed ourselves, & what we make, remake

There were times when this reptile made me quake
But a deeper wonder now I've found
Time reinvents us like a snake

It lives beneath the stairs beside the lake
& eats its mice making not a sound
We shed ourselves, & what we make, remake

I've seen it twice; it shocks you quite awake
Its amazing moves cannot but astound
Time reinvents us like a snake

It used the garage as a dressing room to make
Its presence in absence turn our thoughts around
Time reinvents us like a snake
We shed ourselves& what we make, remake

The day starts; the sun clears the ground
The threat of snow makes the sky's grey haze
Where will you be when the sun goes down?

Off on your journey, ever tightly wound
To gather all in your gaze
Are you coming back from on the town?

Will you call & tell me what you've found?
Or leave me to my own frenetic craze?
Where will you be when the sun goes down?

& where will I be? Might I still astound
Us all, my imaginings ablaze?
Are you coming back from on the town?

I might scale a wall in a single bound
Or find a cure for loneliness that stays
Where will you be when the sun goes down?

In the dark I gather lights around
& animals to nestle in their ways
Where will you be when the sun goes down?
Are you coming back from on the town?

When I was young I wished to be a cat
Years later my cat saved me from despair
I would have died years ago but for that

In later years, death wore a different hat
I courted danger & never had a care
The full moon through the bedroom window…éclat!

Circumstances intervened to make me fat
Medicines & regimes so rare
I would have died years ago but for that

With gratitude forgot, I was a rat
No cat could catch me underneath my chair
The full moon through the bedroom window…éclat!

To those I loved I never was a brat
Put them before me, mortgaged all my air
I would have died years ago but for that

Now I wait, afraid of fortune's spats
That mangle me; watch it waiting there
I would have died years ago but for that
The full moon through the bedroom window: ecat!

I've always been independent & self-styled
The mainstream was a mystery to me
Was there more clarity as a child?

As an adolescent I sometimes dialed
The radio & thought the music was a key
I find my imagination cascades wild

& then when I was married & beguiled
Into thinking self-sacrifice was glee
Was there more clarity as a child?

Could I have prevented horrors, harsh or mild
If I had turned away from some mad spree?
I find my imagination cascades wild

The boss now wants me to "go the extra mile"
& I know that soon they'll shoot me in the knee
Was there more clarity as a child?

Will I ever know if fortune smiled
By making my choices few & all but easy
Was there more clarity as a child?
I find my imagination cascades wild

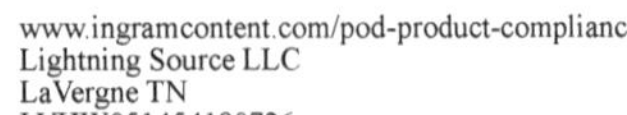